T0067961

LOVE SHOULD IT BE

LOVE SHOULD IT BE

BY

TIFFANY ROGAN

authorHOUSE®

AuthorHouse™
1663 Liberty Drive
Bloomington, IN 47403
www.authorhouse.com
Phone: 833-262-8899

© 2022 Tiffany Rogan. All rights reserved.

No part of this book may be reproduced, stored in a retrieval system, or transmitted by any means without the written permission of the author.

Published by AuthorHouse 03/15/2022

ISBN: 978-1-6655-5468-8 (sc)
ISBN: 978-1-6655-5469-5 (e)

Print information available on the last page.

Any people depicted in stock imagery provided by Getty Images are models, and such images are being used for illustrative purposes only.
Certain stock imagery © Getty Images.

This book is printed on acid-free paper.

Because of the dynamic nature of the Internet, any web addresses or links contained in this book may have changed since publication and may no longer be valid. The views expressed in this work are solely those of the author and do not necessarily reflect the views of the publisher, and the publisher hereby disclaims any responsibility for them.

CONTENTS

DEDICATION

I would like to dedicate a my entire book to Marcus P-Dub Perry, I want to especially dedicate the poem "The Truth" to him because the love we had for each other was very special and very amazing a love I never felt before.

I want to thank Marcus for giving me something no one else has given me a son, our first born child also named Marcus we had together an amazing gift. GOD chose for him to give me the gift of my first born and my only son. We miss him very much. We know he is still with us in spirit watching over us. We love you and miss you very much until we see you again.

LOVE SHOULD IT BE

LOVE IS WONDERFUL

Love is beautifully expressed to us by many different

People that we have met in our lives

Most of the time we don't take enough time out of our lives

To realize how many people have showed us love

Through their actions and not just verbally tell us that they love us

I know that love is truly a wonderful thing to have in one's life

To experience being loved and feeling the expression of love

Love is such a wonderful emotion it can race the clouds away

Dry up the tears that we cried day by day

Love is such a wonderful emotion we can always
depend on it to wash the rain away

<u>LOVE WILL</u>

LOVE WILL MELT THE SNOW OFF
THE MOUNTAINS HIGH

LOVE WILL HEAT THE SAND ALONG THE BEACH SKY

LOVE WILL DRY UP ALL THE RAIN IN YOUR HEART

LOVE WILL LET YOU MAKE A NEW START

LOVE WILL NEVER LEAVE YOU
LONELY AND TORN APART

<u>LOVE</u>

LOVE IS A WONDERFUL THING WHEN YOU HAVE IT

LOVE IS GENTLE AND KIND WHEN YOU HAVE IT

WHEN YOU HAVE LOVE IN YOUR LIFE

YOU FEEL YOU HAVE THE WHOLE
WORLD IN YOUR HANDS

WHEN YOU LOSE IT

YOU WANT TO DIE

LOVE IS PAINFUL ONCE YOU LOSE IT

LOVE IS A MAZE

LOVE IS A MAZE WE WILL NEVER FULLY UNDERSTAND
HOW MUCH THE OTHER PERSON LOVES US
WE HAVE COME TO BELIEVE MANY
DIFFERENT TYPES OF PEOPLE
LOVE US IN OUR LIFE
THAT IS WHY LOVE IS A MAZE
LOVE IS AMAZE BECAUSE WHEN SOMEONE TELLS US
THAT THEY LOVE US
SOMETIMES THEIR ACTIONS MAY NEVER
LINE UP WITH HOW MUCH
THAY VERBALLY TELL US THAT THEY LOVE US
LOVE IS A MAZE BECAUSE WE CAN'T
GET INTO THE PERSON HEAD
TO ACTUALLY SEE WHERE THERE HEART TRULY LAY
LOVE IS A MAZE BECAUSE WE JUST
HAVE TO GO ALONG WITH
WHAT THE PERSON DOES TO
PROVE THEIR LOVE TO US
LOVE IS AMAZE BECAUSE LOVE IS
THE STRONGEST EMOTION
THAT WE WILL EVER SHARE WITH EACH OTHER
LOVE IS A MAZE BECAUSE LOVE WILL TAKE US ON AN
EMOTIONAL ROLLER
COASTERS WE NEVER INTENDED TO TAKE
LOVE IS A MAZE BECAUSE WE FALL ALL IN LOVE TO
BELIEVE LOVE WILL CARRY
US THROUGH THE STORMS OF LIFE
LOVE IS AMAZE WE WILL NEVER BE ABLE TO SOLVE

LOVE IS A BEAUTIFUL THING

LOVE IS A BEAUTIFUL THING

LOVE IS ASSOCIATED WITH ROSES

LOVE IS BEAUTIFUL JUST LIKE ROSES

LOVE HAS MANY DIFFERENT SHADES
OF COLORS LIKE ROSES

LOVE HAS MANY DIFFERENT COLORS THAT
OUTSHINES THE REST LIKE ROSES

LIKE ROSES LOVE IS BEAUTIFUL

LIKE ROSES LOVE HAS TO BE NURTURED

LOVE IS CONTINUOUS FLOWING OF POSITIVE
ENERGY SURROUNDING US

LOVE IS TRULY A BEAUTIFUL THING

ROSES ARE BEAUTIFUL FLOWERS

ROSES ARE BEAUTIFUL FLOWERS

THAT HAS MANY THORNS IN THEM LIKE LOVE

ROSES ARE BEAUTIFUL FLOWERS MEANT TO

REPRESENT LOVE

EVEN THOUGH THE STEM OF EVERY ROSE HAS

THORNS ON THEM

THE STEM ALSO IS PART OF LOVE

EVERYTHING THAT STARTS OFF GOOD MAYBE

DON'T END GOOD

THEN LOVE COULD START OFF ON THORNS AND

WORK IT'S WAY UP TO BEAUTIFUL ROSES

TO SPROUT IT'S BEAUTIFUL COLORS OF LOVE

SOMETHING SO NATURAL THAT BLOOMS

EVERY YEAR

LIKE A ROSE WHEN YOU SEE IT YOU CAN FEEL LOVE

IS NEAR

<u>DREAMS</u>

*D*REAMS WE ALL HAVE DREAMS FOR OURSELVES

*F*OR OUR CHILDREN FOR, MANY PEOPLE WE HAVE
ENCOUNTERED IN OUT LIFE

*D*REAMS ARE SOMETIMES THE ONLY THING WE HAVE
TO HOLD US TOGETHER

*D*REAMS ARE GOD'S GIFT TO US TO
GO FURTHER IN OUR LIVES
THAN REALITY

DREAMS ARE SOMETHING THAT
WE WILL ALWAYS HAVE

NO ONE CAN TAKE OUR DREAMS AWAY FROM US

DREAMS ARE THE FUTURE OF OUR HOPE

DREAMS DEFINE THE FINE LINE OF
PERFECTION THAT WE HAVE
INSIDE OF US

LOVE IS NOT SEX

LOVE IS NOT SEX

SEX IS SEX FEELING OF LUSTFUL PHYSICAL
PLEASURE TO LAST MOMENTARY

UNLIKE REAL LOVE THAT LAST FOREVER

SEX IS ASSOCIATED WITH LOVE VERY OFTEN BUT
THE TRUTH IS

SEX CAN NEVER REPLACE LOVE

LOVE STANDS ALONE

AFTER THE SEX YOU HAVE AN EMPTY NEST

WHEN YOU HAVE LOVE YOUR NEST IS ALWAYS FULL

WHEN YOU HAVE LOVE YOU DON'T NEED SEX
TO MAKE YOU FEEL LOVED

BECAUSE LOVE STANDS ALONE

THE TRUTH

I know a love like I have a never known before

A love I never dreamed I would have the kind of love

That really feels like a fairy tale

This love I know that I have for this man is so intense it is like

A fire in my heart the thought of him keeps me warm

The passion we share continues to follow in my heart

Keeping the memories so fresh in my mind

Our times together the intimate moments we shared together

For so many years are so intense in my mind

I can visualize us together his gentle touch upon my body

The touch of him gliding his hands all over my body

I feel his touch his hands caressing me while I lay next to him

Then he softly whispers to me that we shall never let anyone

Come between our love for each other

I remember all the nights we made passionate love to each other

He left me breathless so many nights

When morning came I didn't want to leave his side knowing

I wouldn't feel the touch of his hands on my body for hours

As I left to go about my day I daydream of his lips upon my ear

Whispering in my ear telling me how much our love means to him

The love we have for each other is so real it has to be the TRUTH

LOVE IS SOMETHING WE ALL WANT

LOVE IS SOMETHING WE ALL WANT

LOVE IS SOMETHING WE ALL NEED

LOVE IS PRICELESS

LOVE CAN'T BE BOUGHT WITH A PRICE

THE BIGGEST DIAMOND RING CAN'T SHOW LOVE OFF

ONCE YOU HAD LOVE YOU NEVER WANT TO LET IT

LOVE IS SOMETHING THAT CONTINUES TO GROW,

WHETHER IT RAINS, SLEET, OR SNOW

BECAUSE LOVE IS SOMETHING WE ALL WANT

IS LOVE FOR A SEASON

If love is really just a season would

That be the reason love tums cold

If love is just for a season would that be

The reason loves folds

If love is just for a season would

That be the reason love is like the wind you feel it to

Sooth you while it's hot then hate it when it's freezing cold

If love is just for a season would that be the reason

We fall in and out love with no regret

If love is just for a season is that why it

Always end in winter when your heart has turned cold

HERE I AM

Here I am without you

Here I am wishing you could hold me

Here I am praying to see your face again

Here I am waiting to see your smiling face upon mine again

Here I am thinking about the good times we had together

Here I am wishing you would come back to me

Here I am laying in this bed all alone waiting for you to come back home

Here I am walking around this house remembering

Us together our vows to never leave each other

Here I am all alone without you

Here I am waiting on you

NEVER

Never is a word we use every day.

Although the word never really don't exist

Never is a word that doesn't carry out its true meaning.

We say we are never going to do something or

Say the wrong things to make us regret the day the words came

out our mouth.

Then we look back on those days.

We have all done our never.

We never said we were going to do.

LOVE IS LIKE TIME

Love is like time when we lose it its gone forever

Love is like time once it's gone we want it back

Love is like time it never moves when you want it too

Love is like time both are priceless

Love is like time we can never go back to recapture either of them

Love is like time it goes at a rate no one can control

Love is like time it never seems to move when we want it too

Love is like time you never feel like you have enough

Love is like time there are always good things that come from them

Love is like time we would give anything
To have them back in our life once they are gone

LIFE AND LOVE

Life is such a wonderful thing.

It comes with such a high price tag attached.

We tend to think life is free.

Life is never free if you want the best things in life

When you love someone, you have to pay the price of

Love a price that we never intended to pay

To live a life day by day has a price to pay

Every day we pay for our decisions we make

Every decision has a price tag we never intended to pay

LOVE SHOULD IT BE

Love should it be something that we all desire

More than life itself

Love should it be something that we believe

We will just die if someone, anyone doesn't love us

Love should it be something that can

Outweigh the storm of live

Love should it be something that controls our

Emotions in every situation in our life

Love should it be something that we can't do without

Love should it be something that is bought with nothing

But cost everything

Love should it be something that knows no end

But have a beautiful beginning

Love should it be something that goes on to send

Us along through the tunnels and channels that were

Forbidden to us

Love should it feel just like love

LOVE IS

Love is full of colors

Love is full of mazes

Love is full of dreams

Love is full of hope

Love is full of truth

Love is full of rays of sunshine

Love is a puzzle with pieces in the sea

Where we will never figure out everything about love

Love is full of all kinds of flowers

But most of all love contains roses because

Roses are the most beloved flower of all that represents love

But it carries many thrones along the way

Thorns that are hidden under the beauty of love

Love is the strongest emotion we will ever have

Love will lead us through the storms of life

And make us forget about the storms we have been through

Printed in the United States
by Baker & Taylor Publisher Services